New York
Deco

NEW YORK DECO

Carla Breeze

Introduction by Rosemarie Haag Bletter

Photographs by the author

RIZZOLI
NEW YORK

FRONT COVER
The grand spire of the 1930 Chrysler Building, designed by William Van Alen, is an art deco beacon at Lexington Avenue and Forty-second Street.

FRONTISPIECE
The polychrome terra-cotta details of the Town House apartments on East Thirty-eighth Street, designed by Bowden & Russell in 1930, contrast with the machined quality of the Chrysler Building.

BACK COVER
The grille above the entrance to Ely Jacques Kahn's Two Park Avenue of 1927 features a golden array of art deco ornament.

For WD-40, the Greatest!

First published in the United States of America in 1993
by Rizzoli International Publications, Inc.
300 Park Avenue South, New York, New York 10010

Copyright © 1993 Carla Breeze
Introduction copyright © 1993 Rosemarie Haag Bletter
Work copyright © 1993 Rizzoli International Publications, Inc.

Library of Congress Cataloging-in-Publication Data

Breeze, Carla.
New York deco / by Carla Breeze ; intro by Rosemarie
Haag Bletter.
p. cm.
Includes bibliographical references and index.
ISBN 0-8478-1552-8
1. Art deco (Architecture)—New York (N.Y.) 2. Decoration
and ornament—New York (N.Y.)—Art deco. 3. Architecture,
Modern—20th century—New York (N.Y.) 4. New York
(N.Y.)—Buildings, structures, etc. I. Title.
NA735.N5B74 1992   91-44140
720'.9747'109042—dc20   CIP

Design by Pamela Fogg
Printed and bound in Italy

CONTENTS

The pioneering work in New York's vast art deco heritage is Cervin Robinson and Rosemarie Haag Bletter's *Skyscraper Style: Art Deco New York* of 1975; obviously, any subsequent work is indebted to this body of research. Don Vlack made a very thorough survey of buildings from this period (the 1920s through the 1930s), published as an index in *Art Deco Architecture in New York: 1920–1940,* upon which I relied heavily for locating more obscure art deco buildings in Manhattan. My other primary source for examples, especially in the boroughs, was Elliot Willensky and Norval White's *AIA Guide to New York City,* and I am deeply indebted to its invaluable research. Alan Balfour's exceptional account *Rockefeller Center: Architecture as Theater,* Andrew S. Dolkart's catalog *Forging a Metropolis,* and Robert A. M. Stern, Gregory Gilmartin, and Thomas Mellins's encyclopedic *New York 1930: Architecture and Urbanism Between the Two World Wars* were also valuable sources of information that I would like to acknowledge.

Producing a body of work such as constitutes *New York Deco* in a city as vast as it is complex requires the assistance and advice of numerous individuals and corporations. To all of these people, I am grateful. Thanks to David H. Neilson of Adler & Neilson Co.; Patrick Clarke of Aleat Construction Inc.; Maureen Tully, John T. Wooster, and Arnold Knapp of American International Insurance (Cities Service Building); the Art Deco Society of New York; Janet Parks of Avery Library, Columbia University; Alan Griffith and Michael Pascal of the Bank of New York (Irving Trust); Lawrence S. Levine and Kathleen Cleveland of Beldock Levine & Hoffman; James Farley of the Chanin Building; William Bassett of the Chrysler Building; William V. Colavito; Petr Stand of Cooper, Robertson & Partners; CSC Partners; John Myles of Day & Meyer, Murray & Young Corp.; Ossie and Julius Decker; Wayne Decker; Baldev Duggal of Duggal Color Projects Inc.; Steven Tole of the Empire State Building; Rob Friedman of Fotocare; Margot Gayle of the Friends of Cast Iron Architecture; Susan Tunick of Friends of Terra Cotta; M. Stephen Klein of the Fuller Building; Cherrie McFadden of Gill & Roeser; George P. Clarke of GPC Advertising; Ernst Wilde of Hasselblad; Loori Grossman of Hudson Park Management; Norbert A. Medenbach and Gene Schmidt of General Electric; Guy Melodia and William Hufstader of Graphic Systems; Howard B. Hornstein; Nina Lavin; Sharon Wheet of Liz Claiborne Inc.; Claire Maida; Michael Downey of the Mendick Management Corporation (Two Park Avenue); Tom Nelson; Andy Udis and Ira Fishman of Newmark Real Estate; Warren R. Bechtel of New Valley Corporation; Myrna Heilbraun of the New-York Historical Society; Diana Goldin of New York Hospital; Merrill Hesch of New York State Historic Preservation; Offermann; Merle O'Keeffe; Renato Danese and Leslie Heller of the Pace Gallery; Syv and Cal Pecker; Richard Perry; Jaime Ramos, Rose Polidoro, Adrian Grad, and Aileen Krikoryan of Radio City Music Hall Productions; Dan Rathke; Allen Daugherty of Red Spot; Bette Engle of Rego Park Jewish Center; Robert Janjigian, David Morton, Pamela Fogg, and Andrea Monfried of Rizzoli; Alan D. Rosenberg; George Voetsch of Rye Playland; Rev. Msgr. Lawrence J. McAlister of Saint Andrew Avalino; Ulrich Krahenbuhl of Sinar Bron; Kenneth J. Quinn of Springer-Verlag; Bernard J. G. Bochtay, editor of the *Swiss American Review;* Jim Cumberland of Swiss Center; Mark Heutlinger of Temple Emanu-El; Rafi Nasser of 275 Madison Avenue (Johns-Manville); Edward Voll of Vertical Systems Analysis, Inc.; Bob Welter; and John J. Wilkins IV.

RIGHT
A dramatic lighting fixture, mirrored in the fillets of the terrazzo floor, soffit lighting, and marble walls create a theatrical lobby for the Fortieth Street entrance of Kenneth Franzheim's 275 Madison Avenue skyscraper of 1931.

NEW YORK AND ART DECO

Rosemarie Haag Bletter

When I first began working on a book on art deco architecture with the photographer Cervin Robinson in the early 1970s, our intention was to cover this phase of American architecture as broadly as possible. We quickly realized, however, that even though much of this work was of comparatively recent vintage—most of the buildings are from the later twenties and the thirties—the vast majority of art deco buildings (with the exception of a few, such as the Chrysler and Empire State buildings) had receded into the larger, anonymous background of architecture that forms the bulk of our built environment.

Yet, art deco buildings should not be seen as "forgotten" architecture, since most were never well-known in the first place. Art deco was not, at heart, an avant-garde style, and for this reason, examples of it were rarely included in histories of twentieth-century architecture. Art deco was not even really a "style" in the traditional sense, but a curiously wonderful mixture of several contemporary styles with traditional and popular undercurrents. It is art

deco's unusual position—somewhere between the high styles of the avant-garde and a full-fledged conservative attitude—that makes it fascinating. Since it borrowed freely from contemporary styles as well as from architectural traditionalism, art deco constitutes a broader reflection of popular tastes and commercial image making than the esoteric innovations of the modernists or the time-honored conventions of the conservatives. Because of its freewheeling borrowing from both groups, art deco was often seen as an unruly interloper and was rejected by both sides.

To include the more populist aspects of art deco, and to cover this period in American ar-

chitecture in general, we became convinced that both comprehensive on-site visual surveys of relatively unknown structures and research of their building permits for dates and architects' names would be necessary in each city and region of the country. We also realized that such an enterprise would take many years and that a basic recording and codifying of a building inventory would best be done by those already familiar with specific cities. We decided, therefore, to concentrate on New York, and especially Manhattan, for our book *Skyscraper Style: Art Deco New York,* which was published in 1975.[1]

We chose Manhattan because art deco, at

ABOVE

Like many art deco buildings, Joseph H. Freedlander and Max Hausle's Bronx County Building of 1934, at Lou Gehrig Plaza on the Grand Concourse, carries a representation of the building—here, for the four entrances, Adolph A. Weinman sculpted maquettes of the structure in the arms of Moses—on the building itself.

OPPOSITE

The massive door frame of the 70 Pine Street entrance to the Cities Service Building (or 60 Wall Tower) is embellished with an accurate model of the skyscraper.

8

least initially, was a sophisticated, urban style. And because we focused on Manhattan in a period that coincided with a boom in the construction of tall buildings, most of the buildings we covered happened to be sky-scrapers, the most obviously remarkable structures of the period. However, although it affected the commercial office building most significantly, art deco was by no means restricted to skyscrapers, and also filtered down to department stores and store fronts, apartment houses, and occasionally even to such conservative building types as banks and churches. But in general, art deco was associated with commercial buildings. Its showy forms—with their eclectic borrowings from futurism, cubism, and expressionism—could be used as an advertisement for modernism, a fashionable collage of newness, without offending the public with the more difficult abstractions of the avant-garde. Art deco remained steadfastly in the realm of the sensual, with its emphasis on lush colors and tactile surfaces.

Since 1975, there have been a number of detailed (and popular) architectural studies of this period. In 1976, Donald Sullivan and Brian Danforth organized an exhibition on Bronx art deco architecture at Hunter College in New York,[2] which dealt mostly with apartment houses built in the thirties and early forties along the Grand Concourse. The style and upscale image of those apartment houses had clearly been influenced by the grand art deco apartment complexes along Central Park West in Manhattan, and the Grand Concourse buildings represent, within the confines of New York City, the gradual migration

LEFT
The wrought-iron door and window grilles of
7 Gracie Square portray the outline of the
apartment building.

OPPOSITE
One reason deco buildings displayed their own
representations was the city's denseness: it was
impossible to see the entire structure from the
street. A panel in the lobby of the Empire State
Building, on Fifth Avenue between Thirty-third
and Thirty-fourth streets, shows its elevation
and location in the New York region.

haps more suited to the decorative arts, it is so widely used today that it would be pointless to retrieve the older terminologies. At any rate, even in architecture one could argue that art deco is distinguished through the use of eclectic, modernistic decorative panels, since the massing and general design of most art deco buildings followed the established mode of American office buildings (as well as the traditional elements of American beaux-arts design, which tended to stress symmetrical arrangements in plan and a clear expression of the building's elevation). There is, in the end, nothing wrong with creating a new term for a development that was never as unified as avant-garde movements, such as cubism, futurism, or de Stijl, and for that reason had never been made coherent under a single name or program. Art deco had no inspired publicists such as Filippo Tomaso Marinetti for futurism or Theo Van Doesburg for de Stijl. *Art deco* functions reasonably well as a label if it helps to make us aware of the importance of the 1925 art deco exhibition as one of the points of departure of a popularized modernism.

10

of a fashionable style from the city center to the outer boroughs. A similar transmutation of art deco took place in the country at large. Aside from several very early important studies of art deco in Los Angeles by David Gebhard and Harriette von Breton, more popular books on Miami, Los Angeles, and Southwestern deco have begun to complete the picture of American regional differences.[3] Carla Breeze has had a considerable role in bringing to our attention buildings that were never intended to be completely anonymous.

Art deco in the twenties and thirties was known as moderne, modernistic, jazz modern, and by several other names. The emphasis then was on its "modernity," not its decorative qualities. *Art deco* came to be the preferred term in the sixties, with publications such as Bevis Hillier's *Art Deco.*[4] The term was an abbreviation of Exposition Internationale des Arts Décoratifs et Industriels Modernes, the 1925 fair in Paris at which the style was popularized and from there disseminated to an American audience. Although *art deco* is per-

While the exhibition brought together, in its various pavilions and displayed designs, an approach one might call art deco, it was by no means a specifically French mode, as some American observers had assumed in the twenties when they referred to it as the "new French style." The dynamic lines of Italian futurism, the sharp zigzag lines of German expressionism, and the measured abstraction of Viennese Secession classicism all contributed to what was perceived as "new" in Paris. In New York's art deco architecture, too, it is easy to detect that wide amalgam of sources: the geometrically stable forms from Vienna, the acute angles from German expressionism, the dynamism from futurism, the collaged effects from cubism; but also geometric abstractions from motifs developed by Frank Lloyd Wright for his California houses, as well as lighting and dramatic presentations from the theater and films. The characteristic art deco design of the twenties suggests sensuous richness, makes use of a wide spectrum of materials and colors, and recalls in its luscious details an older tradition of handicrafts.

Los Angeles, Boston, Philadelphia, San Francisco, and many other cities have office buildings in this mode, reflecting the migration of art deco from Europe to New York, and then throughout the United States. Regional variations often reveal local building traditions of which art deco simply became a temporary expression. For example, Boston's art deco office buildings are comparatively sedate, usually with monochromatic ornament of the same material and color as the stonework of the facade, while buildings in Philadelphia from this period are characterized by lively, colorful, terra-cotta panels. The art deco buildings of Miami Beach, especially those in its South Beach section, consist primarily of resort architecture for middle-class Easterners. The predominant building types are hotels and small apartment buildings, as well as the occasional freestanding house, dating primarily from the thirties and early forties. Miami deco corresponded to the new urban taste for the elegant apartment houses along the Grand Concourse in the Bronx, which here were translated into a white, tropical, and playful style for New Yorkers on their annual winter holidays.

Los Angeles, like Miami Beach, was experiencing rapid development and expansion during this period. But while Miami Beach developed because of the burgeoning concern with vacations and leisure activities in miniaturized urban settings (not quite as alien as the countryside for urban dwellers) away from home, Los Angeles grew in response to permanent settlers and the establishment of the film industry. In Los Angeles, large commercial buildings such as offices, department stores, and movie theaters are strung along major traffic arteries like Wilshire Boulevard. Otherwise, the city is dominated by a strictly low-rise architecture that displays streamlined features, especially in buildings designed during the thirties. This kind of horizontal detailing was not as common in New York's highrise architecture, but is quite appropriate for Los Angeles's low-slung structures, suggesting a city free from tradition, a city on the move.

When studying art deco, one needs to remember that, because of its commercial connections to stylish image making, it was not used in all building types to the same degree. Its major impact was on the office building, the store, and the cinema. The quasi-modern showiness of art deco buildings encountered in a commercial, urban context would have been considered fashionable and entertaining by the same people who might have insisted on a colonial revival style for a house in the suburbs. Similarly, although one finds art deco in the interiors of some urban apartments, especially in New York—the deco apartment on a high floor with terraces hovering above the city became Hollywood's representation of New York, the capital of elegance and decadence, in films of the thirties—art deco was rarely used in the Northeast for the design of freestanding residential buildings, for which traditional styles were generally preferred. A good instance of the conservatism predominant in residential models was the Town of Tomorrow at the 1939 New York World's Fair. The majority of the houses there were meant to evoke a New England village, with only a few of the models designed in a watered-down modern style.[5] In all of the houses, however, the kitchen was sleek and

13

completely up-to-date, while the rest of the interior tended to be more traditional, an attitude consistently reflected in private houses of the period.

Another kind of discontinuity between the external and internal expressions of a building cannot be ascribed to middle-class caution about the image of the home. It springs rather from the personal tastes of the clients of deco office buildings. For example, the robust unruliness of the Chrysler Building reveals that art deco's idiosyncratic forms were used as theatrical devices, but did not reflect the private preferences of the client. Walter P. Chrysler's own office in the building was designed in a neo-Renaissance style, and was insistently conservative. Yet the exterior and the building's public spaces, such as the lobby, elevators, and the Cloud Club at the top of the tower, were extraordinarily brash and luxurious. This dichotomy between private and public taste has a longer, and still continuing, history: Frank Woolworth's office in the neo-Gothic Woolworth Building (1913) by Cass Gilbert was Second Empire revival, with a portrait of Napoleon on the wall. Whereas the exterior of this office building suggested a cathedral—the term "Cathedral of Commerce" was coined for the structure—the private quarters of Woolworth himself were decidedly imperial. More recently, Eero Saarinen's stark, late-modernist CBS Building (1965) contained chairman William Paley's office, which had elaborate wood paneling in the style of eighteenth-century palaces. The disjunction between the private and the public realms in the Chrysler Building is more egregious than that of these other examples

The Lowell

only because of the noisily self-conscious stage-set quality of the public spaces. Dramatic effects were borrowed from the theater during the deco period in other ways as well. For instance, the predilection for elaborate nighttime lighting of buildings coincides with the art deco skyscraper, which was (and again, the Chrysler Building is a good example of this) treated like a prima donna on the urban stage.

Yet another discontinuity exists between the architect's design and his (most architects of the deco period were men) imagination. The competition for the tallest skyscraper—the Chanin Building, Chrysler Building, and Empire State Building were the major players in this particular drama—has often been ascribed to the macho tendencies of male architects. But the competition for the tallest building is probably much more the doing of the client than of the architect. There is in fact visual, if not written, evidence that some architects were at least concerned with the increasing invisibility of extremely tall buildings. With setbacks, most of their upper massing was occluded from the street. Thus, the lower part of the building could be clearly read from the

pedestrian's point of view, but for the most part, the spire was revealed only from a great distance.

In several art deco skyscrapers, this perceptual fragmentation was remedied through the introduction of miniature models of the building near the entrance or in the public lobby space. For instance, in William Van Alen's Chrysler Building (1930), an image of the building occurs in a ceiling mural just inside its main entrance; in Shreve, Lamb & Harmon's Empire State Building (1931), a prominent metal relief of the building is attached to the end wall of the lobby; Clinton & Russell and Holton & George's 60 Wall Tower (the Cities Service Building, 1932) has a three-dimensional model of the building above the entrance; and Shreve, Lamb & Harmon's 500 Fifth Avenue skyscraper (1931) contains a gilded relief of the building held by a mythological figure directly above the entrance. A complete understanding of the particular shape of each building is possible only through these miniaturized representations, as the visual fragmentation in fact increased with the physical proximity of larger and taller buildings.[6] Another remedy for this perceptual fragmentation was less direct and more pragmatic than the representation of the building on the building. This was a greater emphasis on unusual, often polychrome, large-scale ornament on the upper reaches of the structure, near the setbacks and the spire, making that part of the building readable even from a great distance. Ely Jacques Kahn's Two Park

Avenue (1927), with its bright terracotta ornaments, is an outstanding instance of this tendency.

After the stock market crash of 1929, some art deco buildings were seen to completion because they had already been under construction. By the early thirties, however, after the Great Depression settled in, a shift of attitudes as to what was expected of design and architecture occurred, and art deco gave way to the streamlined moderne of the thirties. Architectural imagery in this period depended more on the grayness of the everyday, on science, the notion of progress, and speed as wishful metaphors in a difficult time. As private clients disappeared and the federal government became responsible for the few buildings that were erected during the Depression, the display of luxurious art deco forms became rarer, and monochrome stonework took its place. In contrast to the view of *Machine Age,* an exhibition and book by the Brooklyn Museum that presented the period between the two wars as a unified one, the time was in fact bifurcated by the crash of 1929 and its aftereffects.[7]

When art deco was still used in the thirties, it tended to be in small projects or in the outlying boroughs of New York City, where builders (such as those of the apartment houses in the Bronx) continued to copy the fashionable styles of pre-Depression Manhattan. Carla Breeze has helped greatly to identify many of these lesser-known but evocative buildings in the New York region.

CHAPTER ONE

COMMERCIAL BUILDINGS

Hip flasks, hot jazz, scandal-mongering tabloids, and flagpole sitting—Shipwreck Kelly set the world's record atop the Paramount Theater in Times Square—are as symbolic of New York City in the 1920s as the skyscraper. The essence of American ingenuity and technical precocity was embodied in the city's skyline. Pierced by those "bad boys" of modernism, the Chrysler, Empire State, and Cities Service buildings, New York's silhouette was distinctive.[1] Positive public response to Cass Gilbert's 1913 Woolworth Building was partially responsible for this "skyscraper frenzy."[2] More influential, however, was the 1922 Chicago Tribune Tower competition.

Prevailing stylistic trends, new concepts, and historicism collided in this event. Submissions from American architects were largely in the beaux-arts style, a melange of eclecticism emanating from the École des Beaux-Arts in Paris. Renegades like George F. Schreiber of Chicago applied commercial vernacular solutions in clean, unornamented skyscrapers.[3] Many European submissions, which seemed refreshingly avant-garde, actually recycled American modernism gleaned from the work of Louis Sullivan, John Wellborn Root, Holabird & Roche, and of course, Frank Lloyd

Wright.[4] Howells & Hood's entry was awarded first prize, but it was the designs by Eliel Saarinen, Bertram Goodhue, and Bruno Taut that influenced tall buildings for the remainder of the decade. Ultimately, modernistic design—now termed art deco—superseded historical revivalism as businesses vied to express their commitment to the twentieth century.

The post–World War I decade saw a bull market stampeding Wall Street, the expansion of manufacturing to produce consumer goods, and the proliferation of financial institutions as New York became the corporate nerve center of the United States. American capital was financing the reconstruction of

Europe. Automobiles and radios, among other inventions and technical developments, were producing a heady prosperity. The "economic democracy" envisioned by the Progressive Party was being realized, as every level of society was represented in the economy.[5]

Consumption-oriented industry had evolved simultaneously with Taylorization, with such assembly-line techniques as standardization, centralization, and systematization. Consequently, a demand for other industries like communications and advertising was created, and the innovation that had initially advanced

ABOVE

The lobby and elevator interiors of the Goelet Building/Swiss Center, designed by E. H. Faile at Fifth Avenue and Forty-ninth street in 1931, are virtually intact—astonishing in a city with a mania for interior remodeling—even though they were "modernized" during the 1980s.

OPPOSITE

A popular anecdote regarding Shreve, Lamb & Harmon's 1931 Empire State Building, on Fifth Avenue between Thirty-third and Thirty-fourth streets, told of one of its investors, John Jacob Rascob, who devised the mast because he thought the skyscraper needed a "hat" that could also serve as a dirigible port.

18

technology was absorbed by corporate research and development.[6] Designing and building skyscrapers and large commercial structures was the logical progression of these concepts; after his Tribune Tower success, Raymond Hood envisioned his role as the "leader of the band," orchestrating design, structural and electrical engineering, and other technical aspects into logical forms, such as the slab of the 1929 Daily News Building.[7]

The building itself became a form of advertisement, and endorsement of a modernistic architectural style implied that a company was committed to progress. Recounting a high point in his career, the construction of the Empire State Building, completed in 1931, its contractor Paul Starrett quoted Governor Alfred E. Smith, who had remarked at the time, "You fellows will get a lot of advertising out of this. Think of it, the biggest building in the world, and your name down there on the fence."[8] In 1927, Fred F. French, another contractor-developer, built a lavish brick skyscraper in midtown to represent his empire. On Wall Street, the "giants of finance" alternately scowl and smile upon the public from the City Bank Farmers' Trust Company of 1931; Cross & Cross, also architects of the 1931 RCA Victor Building (later the General Electric Building, now 570 Lexington Avenue), used electromagnetic wave imagery—the zigzag—as a primary motif. Even when unrelated to a specific product, the zigzag became a universal art deco motif, another representation of a company's twentieth-century attitude.

The influence of popular culture on the modernistic style was as significant as that of science and technology. Film and theater sets designed by architects in Hollywood, Paris, and Berlin were widely influential.[9] Less acknowledged is the impact of information conveyed by photography. Black-and-white images, especially of buildings, contained an essentially abstract message; photographing utilitarian brick structures in harsh sunlight could transform three-dimensional reality into jazzy geometrical compositions of strong squares and shadowy triangles. Also, photography itself was inherently contemporary, the confluence of art and technology. Alfred Stieglitz made a major contribution to the popularity of photography as an art form; he also promoted cubist and other nonobjective artists at his Photo-Secessionist 291 Gallery which opened on Fifth Avenue in 1905.

Engineering feats transformed the load-bearing wall into an external skin, affecting the role and type of modernistic ornament. The concept of encrusted decoration became obsolete, and the envelope of a building began to be treated as a fabric, if it was not instead molded by expressionistic tendencies. Ornament was incised or "woven" into the surface in concrete, stone, brick, and metal. Structural and decorative elements—spandrels, headers, transoms—could be mass-produced with prefabricated designs for each building. Discussing these trends, *Architectural Forum* wrote, "This is no doubt due to the recognition of the wall surfaces as the main thing, a plane that is not to be denied, but to be worked in, not upon. . . . Frequently, one cannot tell whether a piece of ornamental detail was inspired by a flower, a figure from animal life, or is purely a composition in line, tone, or color. This is the pronounced

and most salient characteristic of modernist detail."[10]

This type of formal abstraction in the details of architecture and design actually preceded the rise of abstraction in the painting of the first decade of the twentieth century, but the term did not enter popular vocabulary until then. Architect and writer Claude Bragdon, regarded by Lewis Mumford as one of the most influential theorists of the time, played an extensive role in this popularization, as much as the abstract painters themselves, all of whom were also involved in varying degrees with the transcendentalist, or Theosophist, movement.[11] Bragdon's architectural work, while based on harmonic theories, or correlating form with sound, contributed less overall to the art deco movement than did his numerous articles and books. Published in both magazines and professional journals, he expounded theories of geometric ornament, and as editor of Sullivan's *Kindergarten Chats,* Bragdon revived interest in this influential midwesterner's work, who although not overtly committed to transcendentalism had discerned the spiritual implications of the skyscraper.[12]

Drawing upon the work of Walt Whitman, Ralph Waldo Emerson, and William James, Bragdon perceived geometric ornament as

the perfect expression of quantum physics and of the transcendental experience of contemporary life. A 1909 article, "The Skyscraper," urged the use of this type of ornament to impart spiritual values to these "mercenary monsters."[13] Bragdon and others, like the painters Max Weber and Wassily Kandinsky, viewed the fourth dimension as "emancipation . . . from the tyranny of mere appearances."[14] Geometric ornament was the vehicle for the fourth dimension, according to Bragdon. In his books, he analyzed ornament on a "scientific" basis by schematically reducing traditional motifs into grids of "magic" squares and circles, and the accompanying illustrations influenced modernistic decoration.

Ralph Walker, of McKenzie, Voorhees & Gmelin and later Voorhees, Gmelin & Walker, was one of the first New York architects to plunge into this style. Using increased ornament and lavishly wrought grilles, the 1926 Barclay-Vesey Building for the New York Telephone Company expressed the "spiritual and intellectual needs of man [that] can never be satisfied with the thin, austere design of the engineer-architect." Walker added, "The new architecture will not be a thing of slab-sided cubes or spheres, built up of plane and solid geometry in which there is no element of time . . . but will have an infinite variety of complex forms and an intricate meaning that will be comprehensible to minds that are able

to project thought beyond infinity."[15]

Ely Jacques Kahn, by 1928, had already developed a distinctive style. An early masterpiece was Two Park Avenue (1927), done in conjunction with colorist Leon V. Solon. Solon, writing in *Architectural Record,* said, "In place of ornamental subject silhouetted upon its field forming an individual or segregated feature [on the exterior], the motifs are composed of silhouetted repeating forms, superimposed, each treated with a color."[16] Kahn used plastic form to express modernistic tendencies, with projecting brick headers, shadows that created patterns, and motifs woven of vast piers and bands of terra cotta or varying stringcourses. Kahn was more intrigued with exploring spatial and decorative issues on a pragmatic rather than a spiritual level.

Other large architectural firms of the period had their signature styles. Cross & Cross was plainly tied to the beaux-arts tradition, but introduced geometric motifs incised in various materials or cast in terra cotta; the RCA Victor Building was a fling, in which they used richer materials than was characteristic and selected warm colors to reconcile the skyscraper with Bertram Goodhue's neighboring St. Bartholomew's Church. The firms Shreve, Lamb & Harmon, Sloan & Robertson, and Dennison & Hirons all worked in the deco style, and each developed an individual vocabulary. Dennison & Hirons's Chicago Tribune

Tower submission indicates their early commitment to integrating modernistic ornament into the beaux-arts format. Sloan & Robertson were quite prolific, with projects throughout the city.

In 1928, a barometer of significant change, *Architectural Record,* entirely revamped its cover, design, and format to reflect the decline of historicism and the preeminence of art deco. Almost every issue that year was devoted to major buildings in the style, or to associated theories and concepts. The June issue featured one of Claude Bragdon's articles on ornament, this time discussing platonic-solid sources. Numerous skyscrapers, warehouses, manufacturing lofts, and stores were finished that year, and the ground was broken for many more. Slabs and towers, elegant pinnacles and forms began to transform New York into exactly what its visitors had perceived forty years earlier—a symbol of all that was modern, of the achievements of science and technology. The evidence was in the skyline.

The largest hotel in the world when it was built in 1931, Schultze & Weaver's Waldorf-Astoria Hotel takes up the entire city block between Forty-ninth and Fiftieth streets and Park and Lexington avenues. Its articulated elegance dominates the more slender shaft of the 1931 Gothic deco RCA Victor Building (later the General Electric Building, now 570 Lexington Avenue), designed by Cross & Cross.

BELOW

Chevron spandrels with stylized foliation form an overall zigzag pattern on the RCA Victor Building. Cross & Cross was sensitive to the context, especially Bertram Goodhue's St. Bartholomew's Church of 1919, and selected harmonizing warm brick and terra-cotta tones.

25

ABOVE

As on its exterior, the zigzags in the lobby of the RCA Victor Building were intended to convey the ethos of radio communication and the electromagnetic wave. The motif is reiterated in the lobby in sumptuous pink marble, in terrazzo for the floor, and in silver leaf in the ceiling.

The 1926 Barclay-Vesey Building, facing West Street between Barclay and Vesey streets and designed by Ralph Walker of McKenzie, Voorhees & Gmelin, is one of the earliest deco buildings in New York. Its fancifully carved ornament often includes the "bell" telephone logo.

27

LEFT AND OPPOSITE

The "titans of finance" at the second setback of Cross & Cross's 1931 City Bank Farmers' Trust Company on William Street look out over the dense Wall Street district. The forms were no doubt inspired by Theodore Dreiser's novel, *The Titan.*

ABOVE

Ralph Walker, a graduate of MIT, transformed the staid McKenzie, Voorhees & Gmelin when he turned to the modernistic aesthetic for the Barclay-Vesey Building for the New York Telephone Company. The elaborate carvings are featured at each setback.

Ely Jacques Kahn's Two Park Avenue of 1927
expressed the plasticity of the building's "skin"
with projecting stringcourses of brightly
colored and ornamented terra cotta woven
into vertical brick piers.

29

A B O V E

The terra-cotta decoration and color scheme of
Two Park Avenue were designed by Kahn in
conjunction with color consultant Leon V.
Solon. The vivid colors were selected to be
easily read at a distance.

L E F T

The high vaults in the lobby of Two Park
Avenue spring from golden gray marble wain-
scoting and gilt friezes. The ensemble contrasts
flat and highly modeled surfaces, and its fresh-
ness and appeal were admired by writers for
the WPA *New York Panorama*.

ABOVE
The setbacks on the Metropolitan Life Insurance Company North Building, which takes up the full block between Twenty-fourth and Twenty-fifth streets and Madison and Fourth (now Park Avenue South) avenues and was designed by Harvey Wiley Corbett and D. Everett Waid in 1932, are sleekly prismatic.

RIGHT
The polygonal form of the North Building alleviates its solid mass. It was originally intended to have a much higher tower.

Altered for the Foltis-Fischer restaurant chain in 1929 by Erhard Djorup, 411–413 Park Avenue South is an elegant small art deco building trapped between two much larger structures.

BELOW
White plaques that represent architectural elements are embedded into black terra cotta on the facade of 411–413 Park Avenue South.

OPPOSITE AND RIGHT
For the lobby of the 1929 Film Center Building, at 630 Ninth Avenue, designed by Buchman & Kahn, Ely Jacques Kahn again turned to a formal use of color, as he had in Two Park Avenue. But at the Film Center, the technique parodied film imagery as well: black marble strips imitate film; pink marble disks, flush in the floor and projecting on the walls, echo sprockets; and enameled-bronze red dots refer to camera lenses.

ABOVE
The view from a terrace at 29 Broadway includes Cross & Cross's columnar City Bank Farmers' Trust Company of 1931 at the right and a glimpse of the weathered-bronze, pyramidal crown of H. Craig Severance and Yasuo Matsui's Bank of the Manhattan Company of 1929 behind Severance's 50 Broadway of 1927.

ABOVE
The lobby of 29 Broadway, designed by Sloan & Robertson, is sleekly ornamented with embossed aluminum transoms and green travertine, much as it was when it was completed in 1931.

The black-and-white, ziggurat-topped shaft of Walker & Gillette's forty-story Fuller Building of 1929, on East Fifty-seventh Street, appears on the right; at the left is the 1930 Squibb Building, designed by Buchman & Kahn.

35

LEFT
The marble-and-bronze entrance portal of the Fuller Building features an ornate light fixture and a transom, both of polished brass and bronze, and both decorated with foliate motifs.

ABOVE
The pediment over the entrance to the Fuller Building was sculpted by Elie Nadelman; its monolithic skyscrapers represent the business of the Fuller Construction Company.

OPPOSITE, LEFT
After its successful Barclay-Vesey Building, McKenzie, Voorhees & Gmelin (later Voorhees, Gmelin & Walker) continued a long relationship with New York Telephone. This huge structure for the company, a 1932 addition to a 1918 building, on Sixth Avenue between Walker and Lispenard streets, demonstrates Ralph Walker's typical, cleanly articulated approach.

OPPOSITE, UPPER RIGHT
The highly detailed, brick-and-bronze transoms of Voorhees, Gmelin & Walker's 1930 Western Union Building suggest that the building was inspired by Dutch and German expressionism. The structure is on an entire city block in lower Manhattan, fronting on Hudson Street between Thomas and Worth streets.

OPPOSITE, LOWER RIGHT
The Western Union Building is a composition of interlocking forms. The triangular details of the transoms are reiterated in the decoration on the setbacks; nineteen shades of brick were used in all.

ABOVE
The richly adorned lobby of E. H. Faile's 1931 Goelet Building/Swiss Center, with its ribbed marble pilasters, contrasting marble panels, and metal plaques, friezes, elevator doors, and trim, is astonishingly well preserved.

RIGHT
Rockefeller Center, of 1932–40, casts its shadow over Fifth Avenue and the Goelet Building/Swiss Center. Its Associated Architects included Reinhard & Hofmeister, Hood & Fouilhoux, and Corbett, Harrison & MacMurray.

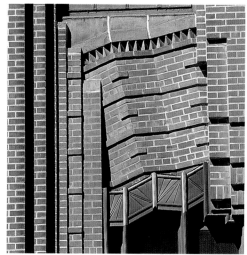

ABOVE
Irwin S. Chanin's private bathroom in the Chanin brothers' own 1929 building at Lexington Avenue and Forty-second Street is typical of the luxury throughout.

OPPOSITE
The Chanin brothers developed housing throughout New York, Times Square theaters (with architecture that promotes fantasy, as well as a classless society), and their namesake building. Sloan & Robertson was responsible for the architecture; the decorative elements, such as the "City of Opportunity" lobby and the lower-level exterior, were designed by sculptor René Chambellan and Chanin in-house architect Jacques L. Delamarre.

LEFT
The owners of Clinton & Russell and Holton & George's Cities Service Building of 1932 wanted a prestigious location, and thus bought property to obtain a 60 Wall Street address, although the building actually fronts on Pine Street. Marble in a number of colors and articulated aluminum banisters ornament the lobby.

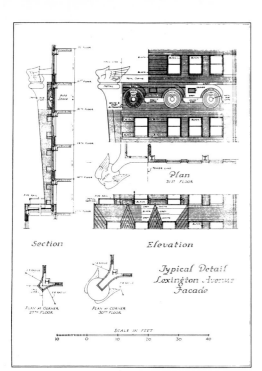

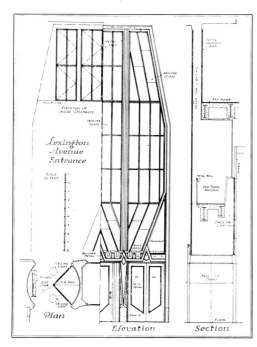

OPPOSITE

The 1930 Chrysler Building was built at Lexington Avenue and Forty-second Street for automobile magnate Walter P. Chrysler, described as a "big man who would not be content in any other city than the biggest." Architect William Van Alen's silver-and-gray stainless-steel composition includes art deco references to both Oriental and Gothic motifs. In addition, the decorative details employ automotive imagery: wheel spokes, hubcaps, and Monel-metal radiator cap gargoyles.

LEFT, ABOVE AND BELOW

Drawings for the Chrysler Building's corner details and Lexington Avenue entrance show the polychrome scheme, the various materials, and especially the automobile allusions.

BELOW

The Chrysler Building lobby was not spared Van Alen's design exuberance, with its lavish walls, floors, and trim, *Energy, Result, Workmanship, and Transportation* ceiling mural by Edward Trumbull, and portrait of the building.

BELOW

The delicate brick detailing and cast-bronze transoms over the side entrances to Howells & Hood's 1929 Daily News Building, on East Forty-second Street, both use stepped-pyramid motifs; the carved panels and lower portion of the transom feature typical art deco ornamentation.

LEFT

The Forty-second Street facade of the Daily News Building was designed with bold white-brick stripes around red-and-black-brick spandrels, and with a three-story granite relief for the main entrance. The relief represents New York, including the Daily News Building; the stripes were criticized at the time, as an overly simplistic ornamental device.

ABOVE AND LEFT
The Irving Trust Company lobby (now a bank-
ing hall for the The Bank of New York) was
one of the most magnificent in Manhattan. The
building, a fifty-story limestone tower at Wall
Street and Broadway, was designed by Voorhees, Gmelin & Walker and completed in 1932.
The rich mosaics, of gold-veined red that shifts
to flaming orange at the ceiling, are by Hil-
dreth Meière, and the sleek brass torchères
create a deco expressionism.

CHAPTER TWO

RESIDENTIAL BUILDINGS

T he endless variety of fronts presented by the better class of tenements and apartment houses in our cities is an endless variety of architectural distress and of suggestions of expensive discomfort. Considered as objects of beauty, the dead walls of the sides and back of these structures, left untouched by the hands of the artist, are commonly the best feature of the building."[1] Thus in 1899, controversial economist Thorstein Veblen in essence predicted the direction of contemporary architecture in his *Theory of the Leisure Class.* In the aftermath of the First World War, his theories were increasingly accepted by mainstream intellectuals and promoted in various progressive magazines such as *The American Mercury* and *The New Republic.* It was ironic that as New York City became the symbol of urbanism's future, the majority of its residents were living in historicist buildings characterized by period revivals, chateauesque apartments, and colonnades.

As land values soared in Manhattan during the postwar period, high-density housing became the only viable means of recouping property investment. Corresponding to the "Cathedrals of Commerce" of business and finance were skyscraper apartment buildings, notably along Fifth Avenue, Park Avenue,

Central Park West, Riverside Drive, West End Avenue, and Sutton Place. The upper economic echelons began to accept the realities of apartment dwellings versus single-family residences, and while much luxury housing was in revival styles, various architects and developers—Emery Roth, Sugarman & Berger, and Irwin S. Chanin—were producing modernistic compositions. The shifting taste was influenced by department store exhibitions of modern interiors. Macy's 1928 Exposition of Art in Industry presented the work of Ralph Walker, Lee Simonson, William Lescaze, and from California, Kem Weber.[2] Lord & Taylor featured similar displays, and the Metropolitan

Museum of Art and the Architectural League also organized exhibitions that transformed the volatile into the acceptable. Joseph Urban's Wiener Werkstätte of America showroom on Fifth Avenue gave art deco design cachet.

As prophetic regarding the appeal of the modernistic style as regarding turn-of-the-century architecture, Veblen noted that objects or ornament that had the appearance of being handmade, even if produced mechanically, would appeal to the more affluent segments of the population, because "ideal precision attained only by the machine . . . would be evidence of low cost."[3] And logically, it was not until the Great Depression, when public-works money was poured into maintaining art

ABOVE
Rosario Candela designed the seventeen-story 740 Park Avenue apartment house of 1931 with Arthur Loomis Harmon of Shreve, Lamb & Harmon. The carved post and finial are typical of art deco ornamentation.

OPPOSITE
Emery Roth, one of New York's principal residential architects of the 1930s, designed this circular, mosaic-encrusted entrance for his 888 Grand Concourse apartment building of 1937 in the Bronx.

44

and craft traditions and their makers (muralists, painters, sculptors), that sleek, machined architecture and interiors became popular.

From the turn of the twentieth century on, New York City's population was expanding by six percent annually, and after the war, a housing shortage affected all its residents. Manhattanites turned to suburbs in Queens and the Bronx where reasonably priced apartments and houses were available, often in more pastoral surroundings. The garden apartment complex, built around a green commons, was appealing in comparison to the vertical congestion of Manhattan. Henry Wright and Clarence Stein designed the Sunnyside Gardens complex (1928) in Queens to provide low-cost housing with the ambience of a single-family residence.

The Bronx became a viable suburb as railroad and subway lines opened vast tracts of land to development. Open space was assiduously protected, and six major parks were within reach of the major new projects along the Grand Concourse.[4] The Grand Concourse was an exciting experiment in the development of apartment housing for professionals and upwardly mobile families. Progressive in terms of layout (two rooms deep versus the single row of rooms in the usual low-cost railroad flat) and amenities (solariums with wheelchair access and supervised playgrounds), apartments built there during the late 1920s and early 1930s represented apartment dwelling at its best.[5] Horace Ginsbern collaborated with Bernard Noonan, an immigrant from Ireland, to fulfill progressive social ideals as well as those of avant-garde design. Ginsbern, who attended Columbia University, although he did not graduate, developed a unique style featuring streamlined forms with modernistic detailing. His experiments in brick, while planer rather than three-dimensional, rival those of Ely Jacques Kahn.

Various legal and financial factors promoted better housing for less affluent New Yorkers. Unions and insurance companies entered residential construction; the Multiple Dwelling Law of 1929 permitted the construction of interior bathrooms; insurance companies were no longer prohibited from investing in housing. Amalgamated Clothing Workers of America, a trade union, was very successful in providing worker housing. In 1927, the Sedgwick Avenue Apartments were built in the Bronx, designed by the award-winning firm Springsteen & Goldhammer. Clarence Stein designed Hillside Homes in the Bronx in 1935, using patterns of brick for ornamental effects. Public housing lagged far behind commercial ventures, however, and standards were actually lowered with the acceptance, under the Multiple Dwelling Law, of mechanical ventilation, which absolved builders from the need to provide air and light in corridors.[6] First Houses on the Lower East Side, completed in 1935, was the first municipal housing project.

Except in the suburbs, residential planning and construction were rarely as attentive to the user as commercial projects, probably because New York has traditionally been a city of commerce. However, by the 1930s concepts of planning, amenities, and art deco design had infiltrated every level of residential architecture in New York.

ABOVE AND BELOW
Horace Ginsbern's Park Plaza Apartments of 1928, at 1005 Jerome Avenue in the Bronx, are lavishly decorated with vividly colored terra-cotta capitals, plaques, and friezes that feature a grand array of art deco motifs. After this early success, Ginsbern designed many other Bronx apartment buildings, most notably, several along the Grand Concourse.

46

Schwartz & Gross completed the magnificently fluted 55 Central Park West in 1930, the end of the era of the avenue's grand apartment houses. The original marquee still shelters the entrance.

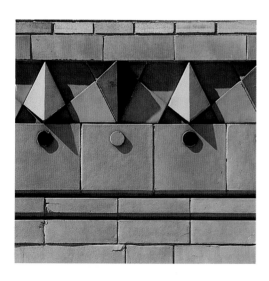

George and Edward Blum, architects of a number of residential buildings from the 1910s through the 1930s, designed 210 East Sixty-eighth Street in 1928. The geometric ornament, in brilliant greens, black, and buff, is all of terra cotta.

OPPOSITE
Bottomley, Wagner & White's River House of 1931, on the East River between Fifty-second and Fifty-third streets, set the standard in both architecture and luxury for apartment buildings that followed. Features include a yacht mooring (since destroyed), automobile entrance court, private riverfront courtyard, and extremely well-appointed and spacious apartments. The Campanile Apartments, at left, were designed by Van Wart & Wein in 1930.

ABOVE
Morris Rothstein designed 7119 Shore Road in Brooklyn in 1930 to take advantage of the corner location. The building has been meticulously restored and maintained.

RIGHT
Black-glazed and buff brick stripes alternate at the entrance to 7119 Shore Road. The etched-glass doors are replicas of the originals.

ABOVE AND OPPOSITE
The Ambassador Apartments in St. George,
Staten Island, designed by Lucian Pisciatta in
1932, are of black and cream brick with decorative elements of intricately modeled and
glazed terra cotta at the entrance and roof line.

RIGHT
The south, 103rd Street elevation of the
Roerich Museum and Master Apartments on
Riverside Drive, designed by Corbett, Harrison
& MacMurray with Sugarman & Berger in
1929, shows the typical massing of skyscraper
apartments in the deco era. The complicated
program included a school, restaurant, theater,
and museum for the works of painter Nicholas
Roerich, in addition to apartments.

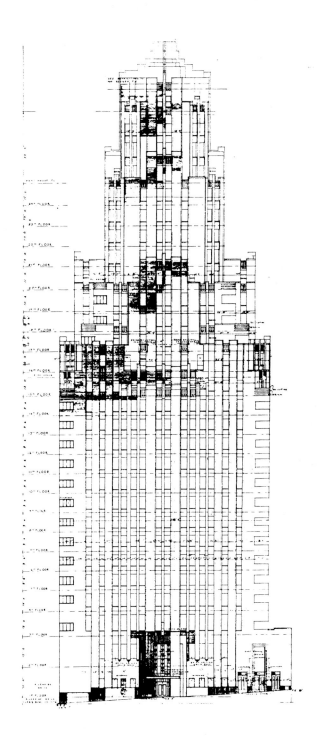

51

ABOVE AND RIGHT
Apartment buildings along Oriental Avenue
in Coney Island, of about 1930 and attributed
to Horace Ginsbern, evoke seaside and nautical
imagery, with sleek, streamlined forms, and
an entrance court featuring terra cotta, etched
glass, and patterned brick paving.

OPPOSITE
The roof decks of the apartments along Oriental
Avenue also recall nautical forms, especially
those of ocean liners, smokestacks, and trellised
open decks.

CHAPTER THREE

ENTERTAINMENT AND RECREATION

It depended on what you read. S. L. ("Roxy") Rothafel, the guiding force behind many lavish New York movie palaces, had been carried out on a stretcher following the opening performance at the building that represented the culmination of his career, Radio City Music Hall, accompanied by either a neurologist (the *New York Times*) or a urologist (the *New York Sun*).[1] Sheets of rain poured on celebrities and guests, like Amelia Earhart, who arrived to partake in the gala December 27, 1932, event. By all accounts the program was extremely lengthy and exceptionally tedious, enlivened only by W. C. Fields, Ray Bolger, and the eminent bacteriologist Dr. Rockwell, who wore his lab coat and "turned scientific patter into comedy."[2]

The inspiration for the interior hemispherical theater design for the technically advanced wraparound stage also varied in contemporary accounts: it was either a vision of Roxy's while on an ocean liner at sunrise or due to the influence of the major theater architect of the period, Joseph Urban. Urban's theater for the New School for Social Research had, in fact, been built just two years earlier. Further complicating the issue, Radio City engineers had visited the Avalon Theater in the Casino com-

plex of 1929 on Santa Catalina Island in California, the first built especially for "talkies," while designing the hall. All of these spaces rely on hemispherical ceiling construction to enhance acoustics. But the experience of Radio City's splendid spaces banished such superfluous cares and concerns. The grand staircase, the gold mirrors, and the luxurious lounges (Donald Deskey was responsible for many of the interiors) made any other consideration trivial.

Roxy had previously worked with theater architect Thomas Lamb; they had pioneered a voluptuous standard of luxury in the Regent and Strand theaters of the early 1910s. For RKO at Radio City, Roxy continued to ex-

plore a new form of entertainment, one specifically designed to enhance talking pictures. Music, dance, and theater formed a hybrid that was initially unsuccessful; under different direction, however, Radio City made a comeback and has been popular ever since.

Theaters are especially vulnerable to development. The Earl Carroll Theater of 1931 at Seventh Avenue and Fiftieth Street is now gone, as is Joseph Urban's fabulous Ziegfeld Theater of 1927. Movie theaters are equally subject to demolition. The Paramount Theater (1926) in Times Square is one of the few that survives as an example of the transition from beaux-arts to art deco, echoed in the progression from first level to pinnacle. The firm responsible for this theater, Rapp & Rapp, went on to design other "baby" Para-

ABOVE
Sculptor Paul Manship modeled turtles and other animals for his 1934 cast-bronze Paul J. Rainey Memorial Gate to the Bronx Zoo.

OPPOSITE
The myriad amusements offered along Rye Playland's midway, in Rye, New York, are sheltered by wooden arcades painted in lively colors; in the evening, they are lighted by the original fixtures.

mounts throughout the boroughs. Unfortunately, the Brooklyn Paramount is now disfigured by storefronts and excessive signage.

In addition to movie palaces, entertainment takes many forms in New York, and also in the surrounding areas. Although reviled for many of his urban strategies and his overemphasis on automobile access, Robert Moses was responsible for building "the finest seashore playground ever given the public anywhere in the world." Conceived on an unprecedentedly massive scale—parking lots for twelve thousand cars, facilities for over fifteen thousand bathers—Jones Beach State Park was little more than a sand bar in 1924 when Moses dragged eminent architects to the site on Long Island.[3] Harvey Wiley Corbett, a member of the design team for Rockefeller Center and Radio City, declined to become involved, and so Moses relied on Herbert Magoon, a young architect with the State Council of Parks, to translate his sketches into reality. But Moses must be considered the true architect of this incredible playground that provided not only cafés, boardwalks, and games, but amenities from clocks on the bathhouses and diaper-changing cubicles to golf and underground passages to avoid traffic.

The automobile and Moses's highways freed people to seek pleasures in the surrounding environs. Another amusement park, Rye Playland, designed by Walker & Gillette in 1927, is just north of New York on the Long Island Sound. Pools and bathhouses, parking and carnival entertainment, a band shell and performance pavilions under the stars were enhanced by the art deco styling of grilles, light fixtures, and ornamentation.

56

·BATH·HOUSE·GROUP·

OPPOSITE TOP
Rye Playland was designed in 1927 by Walker & Gillette as an exotic fantasy. The miradors, minarets, and tiled roofs of the bathhouses and arcades recall the courts and baths of the fourteenth-century Alhambra in Granada, Spain.

OPPOSITE BOTTOM
An elevation of the bathhouse and boardwalk, published in *Architectural Record*, shows the view from the Long Island Sound.

MUSIC TOWER AND BANDSTAND

ABOVE
At Rye Playland, wooden arcades shelter the path from parking to seaside; the beams, posts, braces, and purlins are all carved and brightly painted, creating strong geometric patterns.

LEFT
The focus of Rye Playland's midway is the music tower and band shell, highlighted with shimmering stucco and Moorish motifs.

The Jones Beach bathhouses, designed by
Herbert Magoon in 1929 and 1931, feature a
vast array of nautical and geometric motifs,
including these window grilles and bronze
"waves" on the faux balconies.

59

OPPOSITE
The Jones Beach State Park, a 2,245-acre
public beach—with a huge variety of amenities,
necessary and unnecessary—in Nassau County,
Long Island, was envisioned by Robert Moses
and designed by Herbert Magoon in 1929. The
sleek water tower of 1930 marks a traffic circle
and parking facilities; it was constructed from
very expensive materials (those considered
worthy by Moses), including Ohio limestone
and variegated brick with bronze details.

The Midtown (now the Metro) Theater on
Broadway between 99th and 100th streets is
one of the few art deco theaters that survive
in New York. It was designed by Boak & Paris
in 1933, and features a glazed-terra-cotta
facade and elaborate roundel.

A B O V E A N D R I G H T
The exterior of Starrett & Van Vleck's Down-
town Athletic Club of 1930, at West and Morris
streets, features double-height arcades, salt-
glazed tile in a range of organic tones, and a
cleanly designed marquee. On the interior,
amenities range from swimming and squash to
golf and an enclosed roof garden.

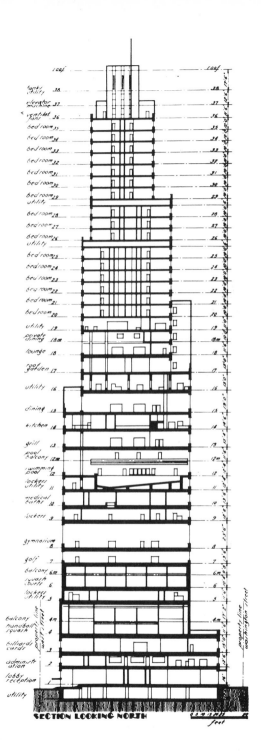

SECTION LOOKING NORTH

62

ABOVE AND RIGHT
The 1932 Radio City Music Hall, at Sixth
Avenue and Fiftieth Street, and its main interiors were designed by Rockefeller Center's
Associated Architects along with New York
theater impresario Roxy Rothafel. The foyer,
with its grandly scaled staircase and balcony,
features sleekly dramatic chandeliers and a
mural by Ezra Winter.

RIGHT

Donald Deskey designed the fresh and elegant lounges, smoking rooms, powder rooms, and Roxy's own small apartment for Radio City Music Hall. Much of the furniture and lighting fixtures was made of cast aluminum and aluminum tubing, relatively new materials in the field. Even the sculpture, *Dancing Girl* by the artist William Zorach, is cast aluminum.

CHAPTER FOUR

PUBLIC BUILDINGS

The needs of New York's growing population were reflected in the constant construction of all types of buildings, but public buildings—courthouses, schools, libraries, hospitals—were the most explicitly symbolic. Regardless of the function of a building, high land values promoted the skyscraper form as the most practical use of space; the associations with spiritual values inherent in skyscraper form and the American lifestyle were especially important for this type of building.

Symbolism also played a significant role in the choice of ornamental motifs for public buildings. The American eagle was reborn in infinite stylized varieties during the 1920s and 1930s, although a publication oriented to architects working under PWA provisions, *The Federal Architect,* disapproved of modernism: "The national emblem should be portrayed with the dignity befitting a symbol of our great national government. It should never be designed or modeled in a grotesque fashion or as a caricature, but in a manner to inspire respect." An accompanying photograph of a geometrically stylized eagle was captioned "grotesque, not indicative of the intended symbolism"; that of a more realistic bird, "refinement in design for plastic material."[1] Cross

& Cross worked with Pennington, Lewis & Mills on the Federal Office Building (1935) at 90 Church Street; its highly stylized eagles, rising from American flag metopes, must have antagonized *The Federal Architect.*

As the Great Depression continued, work and its ethos became dominant symbols, appearing in friezes, murals, and ornamental work. The entrance to the main branch of the Brooklyn Public Library (1941) on Grand Army Plaza celebrates not only history's intellectuals, but also the day laborer. Foley Square in lower Manhattan, like Grand Army Plaza, was for years the subject of planning efforts; its public structures include the New York City

Criminal Courts Building, the Men's House of Detention, and the New York State Office Building, all built from the late 1920s to the late 1930s.

The design of public buildings in other regions of the United States focused on local history, building traditions, and imagery to celebrate a renewed sense of nationalism; in New York, that impetus was never very apparent. Instead, buildings tended toward the streamlined classical variety, except for the magnificent New York Hospital–Cornell Medical Center of 1933, which relied on very schematic Gothic forms and imagery in a skyscraper context. In that sense, New York was a city of the world, representative of American values as a whole.

ABOVE
The streamlined moderne facade of the 1941 Brooklyn Public Library on Grand Army Plaza was indebted to both earlier beaux-arts formalism and to the International Style idiom of the architects, Githens & Keally.

OPPOSITE
C. Paul Jennewein sculpted the gilded bas-reliefs surrounding the library's soaring entrance, and Thomas H. Jones modeled the screen above the doors.

64

66

The circular court leading to an entrance of
the 1933 New York Hospital–Cornell Medical
Center is echoed in the semicircular canopy.
The hospital, a huge complex on the East River
between Sixty-eighth and Seventy-first streets,
was designed by Coolidge, Shepley, Bulfinch
 & Abbott.

The New York Hospital–Cornell Medical Center
was designed in a Gothic deco vocabulary; surrounding the twenty-seven-story central slab
are lower wings, which enclose courtyards.

Stylized eagles, such as this one marking the first setback of the Federal Office Building at 90 Church Street, were often used to symbolize public structures. The Federal Office Building was designed in 1935 by Cross & Cross with Pennington, Lewis & Mills.

ABOVE
This hangar at the Floyd Bennett Aviation Field in southeastern Brooklyn features art deco details. The field was New York City's first municipal airport and the scene for numerous historic flights, including transcontinental speed records.

69

The New York City Department of Health Building (now the Health, Hospitals, and Sanitation Departments Building) of 1935, designed by Charles B. Meyers on Worth Street between Lafayette and Centre streets, is adorned at the main entrance with torchères topped by bronze eagles.

OPPOSITE
Brass transom grilles over the four entrances
to Joseph H. Freedlander and Max Hausle's
Bronx County Building of 1934, on the Grand
Concourse, feature judicial motifs.

ABOVE
A sculptural frieze, the creation of Charles
Keck, runs around the third floor of the Bronx
County Building.

RIGHT
The Bronx County Building is a solid, still
building, unlike many of the dynamically vertical buildings common in modernistic design
in New York.

IF FRATERN
HELD ALL ME
HOW BEAU
THIS WORLDV

OPPOSITE AND RIGHT
Thomas Lamb, the renowned theater architect
who had collaborated with Roxy Rothafel,
brought his usual drama to the 1927 Pythian
Temple on West Seventieth Street. A host of
ancient cultures—Egyptian, Sumerian, Baby-
lonian, Assyrian, Hebraic—along with typical
deco themes provided the motifs for the
facade. Unfortunately, only the ground floor
remains somewhat intact after the temple's
conversion to apartments.

CHAPTER FIVE

ECCLESIASTICAL BUILDINGS

In a period proliferating with "Cathedrals of Commerce," it is almost surprising that an equal number of religious structures were built. With New Yorkers burdened by the stress of modern life, religious observances were perceived as an attempt to "cope with the too-bigness of life."[1] As the pace of living in the 1920s and 1930s eroded traditional practices of religion, ecclesiastical buildings gained a new significance, especially since they met a variety of specialized needs, and not just religious ones. At odds with the one-day-a-week use of a building was the greater emphasis on other activities at the church or synagogue. Sports, clubs, and other ancillary occupations were offered during leisure hours in an attempt to attract a larger congregation, and a certain spirit of architectural competition developed between secular and religious buildings, no doubt resulting from the assimilation of "spiritual" values by advertising and business.

In fact, "the association of business with religion was one of the most significant phenomena of the day." Companies provided religious services for their employees; at a convention for the National Association of Credit Men, for instance, the three thousand delegates had a special devotional service at

the Cathedral Church of St. John the Divine and five other sessions of prayer. A similar coupling of religion and business was evident in Bruce Barton's bestseller, *The Man Nobody Knows,* which argued that Jesus Christ was "the most popular dinner guest in Jerusalem" and a "great executive."[2]

The fervor and competitive spirit of the 1920s are best exemplified by St. John the Divine, which will be the world's largest cathedral, if it is ever completed. Begun by Heins & La Farge at the turn of the century, the church had by 1925 been reworked to reflect Gothic modernism by Ralph Adams Cram.[3] The tower stepped back in the manner of sky-

scrapers; intended to be ecumenical, the church seemed symbolic of the spiritual aspirations of the time.

By the 1930s, the Roman Catholic church was pursuing an important and highly visible construction program in Brooklyn and Queens. Relying primarily on the firms of McGill & Hamlin and Henry V. Murphy, the church had a commitment to modernism that was evident well into the 1950s. Each church designed by these two firms (Henry J. McGill continued alone after Talbot Hamlin left the practice to become librarian at Columbia University's Avery Library) was unique, and

ABOVE

Martin Hedmark's First Swedish Baptist Church of 1931, on East Sixty-first Street, is an early modern design that draws strongly on both art deco and Swedish vernacular traditions, evidenced by this cast-iron sconce.

OPPOSITE

St. Andrew Avalino, a Roman Catholic church on Northern Boulevard in Queens, was largely financed by the Ronzoni family. Although it was designed in the early 1930s, architect Henry V. Murphy did not complete it until 1940. The screen behind the altar is finely crafted from brass filigree; Sienna marble clads the walls of the apse.

uniformly used the best materials and crafts-manship available. Even under tight budgets, either firm could create an appearance that re-lied less on material cost than on design. Mur-phy's National Shrine of St. Bernadette of 1937 invokes Dutch and Danish prototypes such as Peder-Vilhelm Jensen-Klint's facade for the Grundtvig Church in Copenhagen. Murphy's St. Andrew Avalino Church of 1940, on the other hand, is sleekly ornament-ed with black granite and a large brass roundel containing a filigree cross. McGill's work ap-pears more handwrought than Murphy's and uses more cast-concrete ornament.

In Manhattan, there were fewer deco churches and synagogues. Robert D. Kohn, one of the architects of Temple Emanu-El (1929), had been working in a modernistic vo-cabulary since his New York Society for Ethi-cal Culture building of 1910. Even the Church of the Heavenly Rest of 1929 by Mayers, Mur-ray & Philip at Fifth Avenue and Ninetieth Street was more Gothic than art deco. Voor-hees, Gmelin & Walker designed an expres-sionistic faceted facade and auditorium for the Salvation Army on Fourteenth Street in 1930.

Interiors, which are transient and often vic-tims of shifting taste, tend to be the most elusive expression of a particular style. Lobbies of commercial buildings and skyscrapers, for instance, are frequently transformed by the addition of light fixtures, which substitute glaring, even illumination for the original, evocatively moody pools of light and dark. Fortunately, the nature of religion rarely de-mands such alterations, and churches and syn-agogues usually retain their original interiors, with few changes.

76

OPPOSITE
The stained glass in St. Andrew Avalino's radiating chapels was fabricated by Daprato Studios.

LEFT
Anthropomorphic lions guard St. Andrew Avalino's incised-brass entrance doors.

BELOW
The exterior of St. Andrew Avalino, with its brass roundel and filigree cross, is as abundantly ornamented as its interior.

OPPOSITE
The National Shrine of St. Bernadette, Henry
V. Murphy's 1937 design on Thirteenth Avenue
in southwestern Brooklyn, owes a debt to
Dutch expressionism, with its inventively ma-
nipulated exterior materials, brick and copper.

ABOVE
A grotto next to the chapel at St. Bernadette
holds her statue; the grotto motif is used inside
the sanctuary as well.

LEFT
St. Bernadette also appears in a muted terra-
cotta lintel over the rectory house entrance.

ABOVE
Carved limestone angels encircle the campanile of the Blessed Sacrament Church complex—church, convent, and auditorium—on Thirty-fifth Avenue in central Queens. The campanile is part of the church, designed by Henry J. McGill in 1949 as the last part of the complex.

RIGHT
Before the church, at left, Henry J. McGill had designed the auditorium for Blessed Sacrament, at right, with his partner Talbot Hamlin in 1933, and its convent, at center, on his own in 1937, after Hamlin became librarian for Avery Library at Columbia University.

The architects of the 1929 Temple Emanu-El at Fifth Avenue and Sixty-fifth Street—Kohn, Butler & Stein with Mayers, Murray & Philip—are identified on the plaque in its entrance foyer, along with its trustees and building committee. The rich materials of the foyer are softly lighted by torchères.

ABOVE
The Rego Park Jewish Center, which is on Queens Boulevard in central Queens, was designed in 1941 by the architect Frank Grad.

RIGHT, ABOVE AND BELOW
The decorative elements at the Rego Park Jewish Center—including a mosaic mural over the entrance and interior stained glass—portray symbols of the Jewish faith.

CHAPTER SIX

PINNACLES

When he wrote about the Empire State Building, Paul Starrett rightfully titled the chapter on its pinnacle "The Climax."[1] Being at the pinnacle of a skyscraper is exhilarating—the wind sweeps the air clean; masses of people seem insignificant; unimaginable space opens up—and building such edifices gives a great sense of power and possession. Architect Cass Gilbert wrote, "These vast buildings have grown up in less than a generation, many of them marvels of ingenuity in design and equipment, and all of them combining into masses and groups of rare beauty. Color, form, ornament, all play their part in the great picture. They rise into the morning sunlight with new glory each day, fresh, sparkling, joyous, as it were, to proclaim the stirring vitality of the surging throng of humanity passing in and out of this great gateway of commerce. As the evening falls, the higher towers, gilded by the rays of the setting sun, reflect new splendors of color and light; while from their myriad windows the purpling mists of advancing night are illuminated with a million glittering stars."[2]

Often concealing mechanical equipment, the pinnacle was a building's signature. It was here that a building gained advertising prestige

and set itself apart from its neighbors, and as much attention was lavished on this portion of the building as on the ground level and lobby. What from afar seems to be perfectly balanced is massive upon close contact.

The most commonly used materials were terra cotta and metal. Both could be colored and given any form or pattern. Said a promotional brochure at the time, "A terra-cotta roof is not only interesting and beautiful, but thoroughly practical and watertight. . . . American architecture . . . is establishing its own precedents in design and color."[3]

The sources for many pinnacles may be found in the Chicago Tribune Tower compe-

tition; some are more pragmatic than others. Also, sexual associations between skyscrapers and the cult of the phallic are unavoidable. These were buildings built by men, since there were few women architects at the time. Certainly the architects themselves were aware of the overt symbolism, and perhaps for this reason emphasized spiritual implications instead, as Louis Sullivan did when he said, "The tall office building . . . must be every inch a proud and soaring thing."[4] Most building tops were squared, lancet, or lanternate; some were columnar or prismatic, like the City Bank Farmers' Trust and Irving Trust (1932) in the Wall Street district. Whatever the impetus, the skyscraper pinnacle made New York City's skyline unique during the jazz era.

ABOVE

The pinnacle and dome at Rye Playland, Walker & Gillette's 1927 seaside escape in Rye, New York, were described in _Architectural Record_ as a design "with an entirely new feeling."

OPPOSITE

The pinnacle of the Gothic deco RCA Victor Building (later the General Electric Building, now 570 Lexington Avenue) soars fancifully into the sky, energized by its carvings, gilding, and dynamic electromagnetic zigzags.

87

A B O V E
The Paramount Building in Times Square, housing the Paramount Theater (both designed by Rapp & Rapp in 1926), embodies in its architecture the change from beaux-arts to art deco. The glass globe and clock face were lighted at night.

R I G H T
The band shell at Rye Playland, designed by Walker & Gillette in 1927, has a prismatic, glass-and-metal tower that shimmers in the seaside light.

O P P O S I T E
While the original sparkling glass tiles at the pinnacle of Central Park South's Barbizon Plaza Hotel, designed by Murgatroyd & Ogden in 1930, were unfortunately reclad in gold, the sleek surface does recall the deco aesthetic.

OPPOSITE
The top of Bottomley, Wagner & White's 1931
River House, which faces the East River between Fifty-second and Fifty-third streets,
shows the contrast between art deco's hand-
crafted aspect and its machined look: the
highly polished and finished spire of the
Chrysler Building.

ABOVE
The Newsweek Building at 444 Madison
Avenue, designed by Kohn, Vitola & Knight
in 1931, has a strong geometric pinnacle.

LEFT
The blue-green terra-cotta panels of the 1931
McGraw-Hill Building on West Forty-second
Street, by Raymond Hood, Godley & Fouilhoux,
are treated with sleek horizontality at the top.

OVERLEAF
Sugarman & Berger's New Yorker Hotel of
1930, on Eighth Avenue between Thirty-fourth
and Thirty-fifth streets, was one of the city's
largest; although the building is no longer a
hotel, the sign still announces it proudly.

Introduction

1. Cervin Robinson and Rosemarie Haag Bletter, *Skyscraper Style: Art Deco New York* (New York: Oxford University Press, 1975). The same year, the Brooklyn Museum organized an exhibition of that title guest curated by Bletter and Robinson. Between 1975 and 1977, the exhibit traveled to numerous museums in the Northeast and the Midwest.

2. Donald Sullivan and Brian Danforth, "Bronx Art Deco Architecture" (unpublished exhibition catalog, Graduate Program in Urban Planning, Hunter College, City University of New York, 1976).

3. David Gebhard and Harriette von Breton, *Kem Weber: The Moderne in Southern California 1920 through 1941* (Santa Barbara: The Art Galleries, University of California, 1969); David Gebhard and Harriette von Breton, *L.A. in the Thirties 1931–1941* (Salt Lake City: Peregrine Smith, 1975); Carla Breeze, *L.A. Deco* (New York: Rizzoli, 1991); Laura Cerwinske, *Tropical Deco: The Architecture and Design of Old Miami Beach* (New York: Rizzoli, 1981); Carla Breeze, *Pueblo Deco* (New York: Rizzoli, 1990); Marcus Whiffen and Carla Breeze, *Art Deco Architecture of the Southwest* (Albuquerque: University of New Mexico Press, 1984); Hans Wirz and Richard Striner, *Washington Deco: Art Deco in the Nation's Capitol* (Washington, D.C.: Smithsonian, 1984).

4. Bevis Hillier, *Art Deco* (London: Studio Vista, 1968). For a more comprehensive bibliography, see also Bevis Hillier, *The World of Art Deco* (exhibition catalog, Minneapolis Institute of Arts, 1971).

5. Rosemarie Haag Bletter, "The World of Tomorrow: The Future with a Past," *High Styles: Twentieth-Century American Design* (New York: Whitney Museum of American Art/Summit Books, 1985), 84–127.

6. Rosemarie Bletter, "Metropolis réduite," *Archithese* 18 (1976): 22–27.

7. Richard Guy Wilson, Dianne H. Pilgrim, and Dickran Tashjian, *The Machine Age in America 1918–1941* (New York: Abrams, 1986).

Chapter 1

1. "Can Modern Architecture Be Good?" *The Federal Architect,* October 1930, 6.

2. New York City Historic Landmark plaque, Empire State Building, 1976.

3. Howard L. Cheney, Advisory Architect, *The International Competition for a New Administration Building for the Chicago Tribune MCMXXII* (Chicago: The Tribune Company, 1923; reprint, Stanley Tigerman, *Chicago Tribune Tower Competition & Late Entries,* New York: Rizzoli, 1981).

4. Claude Bragdon, *The Frozen Fountain* (New York: Alfred A. Knopf, 1932), 23.

5. Frederic Lewis Allen, *Only Yesterday: An Informal History of the 1920's* (New York: Harper & Row, 1931), 137.

6. Thomas P. Hughes, *American Genesis: A Century of Invention and Technological Enthusiasm 1870–1970* (New York: Viking Penguin, 1989), 159.

7. Alfred C. Bossom, *Building to the Skies: The Romance of the Skyscraper* (London: Studio, 1934), 55.

8. Paul Starrett with Webb Waldron, *Changing the Skyline* (New York: McGraw Hill, 1938), 289.

9. Robinson and Bletter, *Skyscraper Style,* 64.

10. Parker Morse Hooper, "Modern Architectural Decoration," *Architectural Forum,* February 1928, 158.

11. Linda Dalrymple Henderson, "Mysticism, Romanticism, and the Fourth Dimension," in *The Spiritual in Art: Abstract Painting 1890–1985,* ed. Maurice Tuchman (New York: Los Angeles County Museum of Art/Abbeville Press, 1986), 220.

12. Lewis Mumford, *Roots of Contemporary Architecture* (New York: Dover Publications, 1972), 422.

13. Claude Bragdon, "Architecture in the United States: The Skyscraper," *Architectural Record,* August 1909, 84.

14. Claude Bragdon, *Architecture and Democracy* (New York: Alfred A. Knopf, 1918), 103.

15. Ralph Walker, "A New Architecture," *Architectural Forum,* January 1928, 3, 4.

16. Leon V. Solon, "The Park Avenue Building, New York City: The Evolution of a Style," *Architectural Record,* April 1928, 296.

Chapter 2

1. Thorstein Veblen, *The Theory of the Leisure Class: An Economic Study of Institutions* (1899; reprint, New York: Viking Press, 1931), 154.

2. "The Macy Exposition of Art in Industry," *Architectural Record,* August 1928, 137.

3. Veblen, *Theory of the Leisure Class,* 160.

4. Sullivan and Danforth, "Bronx Art Deco Architecture," 4.

5. Sullivan and Danforth, "Bronx Art Deco Architecture," 47.

6. Robert A. M. Stern, Gregory Gilmartin, and Thomas Mellins, *New York 1930: Architecture and Urbanism Between the Two World Wars* (New York: Rizzoli, 1987), 417, 486, 444.

Chapter 3

1. *New York Sun* article, Radio City Music Hall scrapbook, n.d.

2. Brooks Atkinson, "The Play: Music Hall's Opening," *New York Times,* December 28, 1932, 14.

3. Robert A. Caro, *The Power Broker: Robert Moses and the Fall of New York* (New York: Vintage Books, 1974), 309, 223.

Chapter 4

1. Arthur L. Blakeslee, "Symbolism on Federal Buildings: The Eagle," *The Federal Architect,* July 1933, 12.

Chapter 5

1. Robert S. Lynd and Helen Merrell Lynd, *Middletown* (New York: Harcourt, Brace & Company, 1929), 315.

2. Allen, *Only Yesterday,* 148.

3. Stern, Gilmartin, and Mellins, *New York 1930,* 155.

Chapter 6

1. Starrett and Waldron, *Changing the Skyline,* 284.

2. Cass Gilbert, "Introduction," in Vernan Howe Batley, *Skyscrapers of New York* (New York: William Edwin Rudge, 1928).

3. "Terra Cotta Towers," *Atlantic Terra Cotta,* January 1928, 1.

4. Louis H. Sullivan, "The Tall Office Building Artistically Considered," *Western Architect,* vol. 31, no. 1 (1896): 4.

Balfour, Alan. *Rockefeller Center: Architecture as Theater*. New York: McGraw-Hill, 1978.

Banham, Reyner. *Theory and Design in the First Machine Age*. London: The Architectural Press, 1960.

Bragdon, Claude. *Architecture and Democracy*. New York: Alfred A. Knopf, 1926.

———. *Four-Dimensional Vistas*. New York: Alfred A. Knopf, 1916.

———. *The Frozen Fountain*. New York: Alfred A. Knopf, 1932.

———. *More Lives than One*. New York: Alfred A. Knopf, 1938.

Cheney, Sheldon. *A Primer of Modern Art*. New York: Boni & Liveright, 1924.

Cochran, Thomas C., and William Miller. *The Age of Enterprise: A Social History of Industrial America*. 1942. Reprint. New York: Harper & Row, 1961.

Conrad, Peter. *The Art of the City: Views and Visions of New York*. New York: Oxford University Press, 1984.

Dearstyne, Howard. *Inside the Bauhaus*. New York: Rizzoli, 1986.

Dolkart, Andrew S. *Forging a Metropolis*. New York: Whitney Museum of American Art, 1990.

Federal Writers' Project. *New York Panorama*. New York: Pantheon, 1984.

Fitch, James Marston. *American Building: The Historical Forces That Shaped It*. Boston: Houghton Mifflin, 1948.

Gill, Brendan. *Many Masks: A Life of Frank Lloyd Wright*. New York: G. P. Putnam's Sons, 1987.

Goldberger, Paul. *The City Observed: New York*. New York: Random House, 1979.

Goldman, Jonathan. *The Empire State Building Book*. New York: St. Martin's Press, 1980.

Hayden, Dolores. *The Grand Domestic Revolution: A History of Feminist Designs for American Homes, Neighborhoods, and Cities*. Cambridge: MIT Press, 1981.

Henderson, Linda Dalrymple. *The Fourth Dimension and Non-Euclidean Geometry In Modern Art*. Princeton: Princeton University Press, 1983.

Homer, William I. *Alfred Stieglitz and the American Avant-Garde*. Boston: New York Graphic Society, 1977.

James, William. *The Varieties of Religious Experience*. New York: The Modern Library, 1936

Kilham, Walter H. *Raymond Hood, Architect; Form Through Function—The American Skyscraper*. New York: Architectural Book Publishing Co., 1973.

Kouwenhoven, John A. *Made in America*. New York: Doubleday, 1948.

Lane, Wheaton J. *From Indian Trail to Iron Horse*. Princeton: Princeton University Press, 1939.

Leuchtenburg, William E. *The Perils of Prosperity, 1914–1932*. Chicago: University of Chicago Press, 1958.

Lichtenberg, Bernard. "Advertising Campaigns." *Modern Business Tracts* XIII. (New York: Alexander Hamilton Institute, 1926).

Limber, Ralph C. "Economic and Technological Change in American Agriculture in Relation to Crop Land Requirements." Ph.D. diss., New York University, 1942.

Lynd, Robert S., and Helen M. *Middletown*. New York: Harcourt, Brace and Company, 1929.

———. *Middletown in Transition*. New York: Harcourt, Brace and Company, 1937.

Menocal, Narisco G. *Architecture as Nature: The Transcendentalist Idea of Louis Sullivan*, Madison: University of Wisconsin Press, 1981.

Morrison, Hugh S. *Louis Sullivan: Prophet of Modern Architecture*. New York: W. W. Norton, 1935.

Mumford, Lewis. *The Culture of Cities*. New York: Harcourt, Brace and Company, 1938.

———. *Technics and Civilization*. New York: Harcourt, Brace and Company, 1934.

Nevins, Allan. *Ford*. 3 vols. New York: Scribners & Sons, 1954, 1957, 1963.

———. *John D. Rockefeller*. 2 vols. New York: C. Scribners Sons, 1940.

Norman, Dorothy. *Alfred Stieglitz: An American Seer*. New York: Aperture, 1973.

Park, Edwin Avery. *New Backgrounds for a New Age*. New York: Harcourt, Brace and Company, 1927.

Pehnt, Wolfgang. *Expressionist Architecture*. London: Thames & Hudson, 1973.

Presbrey, Frank. *The History and Development of Advertising*. New York: Doubleday, 1929.

Raney, William F. *Wisconsin Inc., A Story of Progress*. New York: Prentice-Hall, 1940.

Recent Social Trends in the United States. Report of the President's Committee on Social Trends. New York, London: McGraw-Hill Book Company, Inc., 1934.

Ripley, William Z. *Main Street and Wall Street*. Boston: Little, Brown and Co., 1927.

Robinson, Cervin, and Rosemarie Haag Bletter. *Skyscraper Style: Art Deco New York*. New York: Oxford University Press, 1975.

Sexton, R. W. *American Public Buildings of Today*. New York: Architectural Book Publishing Company, Inc., 1931.

Soule, George. *Prosperity Decade; From War to Depression, 1917–1929*. New York: Rinehart Press, 1947.

Stern, Robert A. M., Gregory Gilmartin, and Thomas Mellins. *New York 1930: Architecture and Urbanism Between the Two World Wars*. New York: Rizzoli, 1987.

Sullivan, Donald, and Brian Danforth. "Bronx Art Deco Architecture." Unpublished exhibition catalog, Graduate Program in Urban Planning, Hunter College, City University of New York, 1976.

Tarbell, Ida M. *The History of the Standard Oil Company*, vol. 1. New York: Peter Smith. 1925.

———. *The Nationalizing of Business, 1878–1898*. New York: The Macmillan Company, 1936.

Troy, Nancy J. *Modernism and the Decorative Arts in France: Art Nouveau to Le Corbusier*. New Haven: Yale University Press, 1991.

——— and Sergei Eisenstein. *Film Form*. New York: Harcourt, Brace and Company, 1949.

Tuchman, Maurice, ed. *The Spiritual in Art: Abstract Painting 1890–1985*. New York: Los Angeles County Museum of Art/Abbeville Press, 1986.

Tunnard, Christopher, and Henry H. Reed. *American Skyline*. Boston: Houghton Mifflin, 1955.

Van Leeuwen, Thomas A. P. *The Skyward Trend of Thought: The Metaphysics of the American Skyscraper*. Cambridge: MIT Press, 1988.

Vlack, Don. *Art Deco Architecture in New York: 1920–1940*. New York: Harper & Row, 1974.

Weber, Max. "The Fourth Dimension from a Plastic Point of View." *Camera Work* 31 (July 1910).

Willensky, Elliot, and Norval White. *AIA Guide to New York City*. 3rd ed. New York: Harcourt Brace Jovanovich, Publishers, 1988.

Wright, Frank Lloyd. *Studies and Executed Buildings by Frank Lloyd Wright*. New York: Rizzoli, 1986. Reprint of the Wasmuth portfolio, 1910.

95

The Irving Trust Company lobby of 1932.